FRIESIAN HORSES

For a free color catalog describing Gareth Stevens' list of high-quality books, call 1-800-542-2595 (USA) or 1-800-461-9120 (Canada). Gareth Stevens' Fax: (414) 225-0377.

Library of Congress Cataloging-in-Publication Data available upon request from publisher.
Fax: (414) 225-0377 for the attention of the Publishing Records Department.

ISBN 0-8368-1368-5

This edition first published in North America in 1995 by
Gareth Stevens Publishing
1555 North RiverCenter Drive, Suite 201
Milwaukee, Wisconsin 53212, USA

First published in Great Britain in 1994 by Sunburst Books, Deacon House, 65 Old Church Street, London, SW3 5BS.
Photographs © 1989 Franckh'sche Verlagshandlung, W. Keller & Co., Stuttgart, Germany. Text © 1994 Sunburst Books.
Additional end matter © 1995 by Gareth Stevens, Inc.

U.S. Series Editor: Patricia Lantier-Sampon
U.S. Editor: Barbara J. Behm

Printed in China

1 2 3 4 5 6 7 8 9 99 98 97 96 95

FRIESIAN HORSES

Photography by
Tomáš Míček

Text by
Dr. Hans-Jörg Schrenk

Gareth Stevens Publishing
MILWAUKEE

A Friesian stallion trots imposingly across a meadow. He makes it clear, through his arched neck and erect tail, that this is his territory.

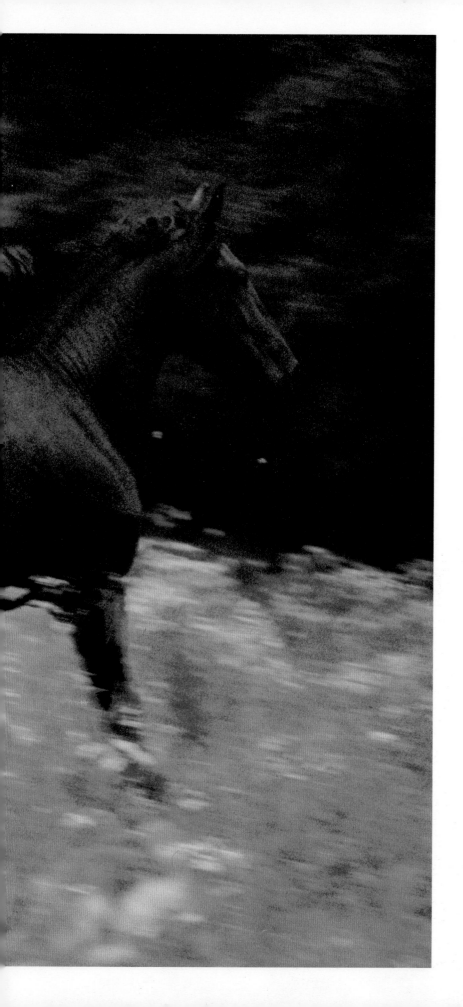

Whether Friesian horses are in a parade carrying riders in historical costume or as part of a classical team pulling a carriage, they are admired by horse lovers everywhere. These magnificent horses awaken memories of times gone by when they were used primarily for parades and to demonstrate complicated dressage movements.

Two young stallions. Friesians are black beauties with long, thick manes and silky coats.

Horses have been bred in Friesland, a province in northern Holland, for over two thousand years. Today's Friesians were influenced by crossbreeding with Andalusian horses in the sixteenth and seventeenth centuries, at the time of the Spanish occupation of the Netherlands. During that time, Friesian horses were gaining a reputation not only as ideal dressage horses, but also as war horses. In the seventeenth century, there were strict rules for breeding Friesians, and the horses flourished. But around the middle of the nineteenth century, Friesians began to lose the value they had once known. Buyer requirements at that time were for heavy horses to work the land. The Friesians, therefore, seemed doomed to die out.

Friesians have inherited the strong neck, long mane, and high-stepping gait of the Andalusian horses.

8

Friesian mares with their foals. The Friesian is one of the oldest of all the European breeds.

*Friesians were popular during medieval times. Knights were grandly
mounted on these showy, black horses.*

Mares and foals gaze at the camera. The foals' coats are still tinged with brown and will gradually turn a glossy black as the foals get older.

12

Wide open meadowlands are necessary to breed healthy foals.

By growing up in a herd, the horses learn to get along with each other and to respect the herd's hierarchy.

15

In 1878, a group of Friesian horse breeders formed a society with the aim of preventing the original Friesian race from dying out. The original breeding records of this society listed 8 Friesian stallions and 10 mares. By 1896, the stock had grown to 133 mares and 7 stallions. In 1913, the horses took a turn downward with only 3 stallions. To save the race, another society was formed to monitor the quality of the horses. As a result, the Friesians today are popular leisure horses, well suited to both riding and driving in harness. Many breeding areas throughout the world have been added to the original one in Friesland, particularly in the United States, Australia, and Germany.

When horses are kept in herds, friendships often grow between two animals that can last for years. The two will usually stand close to one another when resting or dozing, eat together, and take care of each other's coat-grooming needs.

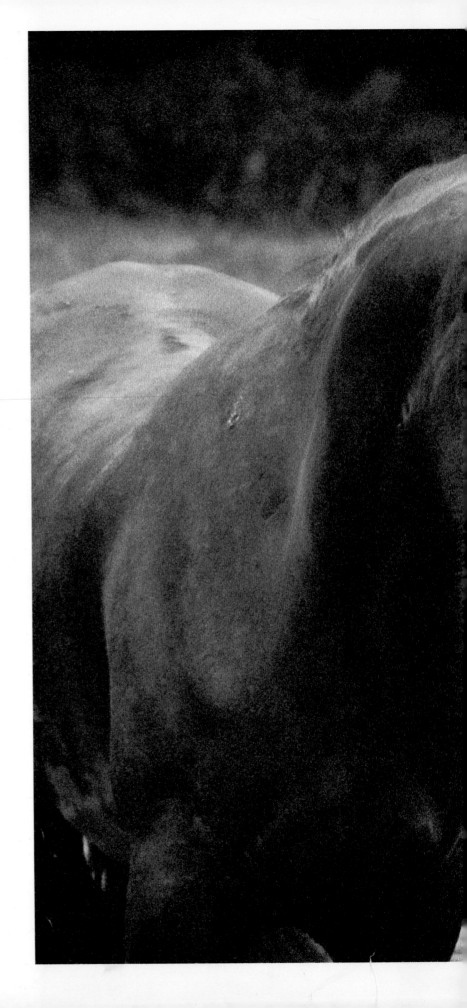

*This foal is cautiously edging closer to an unknown mare, until he can
get to know her scent. In the first few days of life, foals do not dare
stray far from their mothers. It is only when they are a few
weeks old that foals will roam a little bit and
approach unfamiliar mares.*

But a foal will always return to its mother for a drink of milk. At first, foals nurse every half hour, then later, every hour. At the age of six to eight months, they are separated from their mothers.

This stallion demonstrates the high knee action that the Friesians inherited from their Andalusian ancestors.

On the following pages: Young stallions have a certain behavior pattern in which they alternate eating and playing with rest periods. During times of rest, the horses very rarely fall into a deep sleep. Most of the time, they just doze.

21

*This mare surveys her surroundings. Her ears, alert and forward,
point toward something that has caught her attention.*

Playing is always interrupted by breaks, either to graze or rest.

The wide brow and long, silky forelock are distinguishing features of the Friesian.

27

A stallion sniffs in vain at a gelding.

The gelding remains undisturbed by the stallion, despite the stallion's impressive stance and the blow from his foreleg.

Friesian stallions used for breeding have to meet strict requirements established by the breeders' union. At the age of three, stallions must stand at least 59-63 inches (about 1.58 meters) high. If they meet this requirement, they then must undergo various performance tests for both riding and driving. They are also judged on their character and training capacity. Even if the stallion passes all the tests, he still receives just a temporary breeding license, valid for only one year. At the end of the year, the stallion's offspring are examined. If the foals appear to have inherited good genes, then the stallion is granted a license for breeding that is valid for several years. The goal of Friesian breeders is to rear a strong horse with an elegant, arched neck; a broad chest; a slightly divided croup; and muscular hindquarters. Equally important are the long mane, thick tail, and glossy coat. Today's thoroughbred Friesians are completely black.

This struggle between two stallions may look dangerous, but it is not. The fact that the ears of both horses are pointing forward means this is not a serious fight.

During this play-fight, one of the stallions draws himself up, while the other tries to bite his chest.

Then the other stallion also rears up on his hindquarters to dodge the blows of his opponent.

In between games, the horses always take short pauses to catch their breath. Here each of the stallions waits to see if the other is going to resume the play-fight.

There are three different types of Friesian horses. The most heavily built and stocky type has very pronounced joints and is well muscled overall. This type is an ideal carriage horse and suited for heavy farm work. It is distinguished from the other types by its high knee action and energetic gait. The mid-weight type represents the ideal goal for most breeders. This type has a small head, glossy coat, wide chest, and high, arched neck. This horse is ideal for both carriage driving and riding. The third type of Friesian is lighter and has longer legs. It is very fast and light on its feet, making it the perfect horse for competitive sports.

Yet again, the two opponents rear up on their forelegs, locking together like wrestlers.

When one of the fighters turns away and starts to graze, the other flings up his head and flares his nostrils, probably picking up the scent of a nearby mare.

Friesians have long heads with expressive, alert eyes.

These horses are spirited, but easily trained. They have a willing, gentle character.

Two mares groom each other. This kind of skin care routine usually takes place when the horses are resting at midday.

Friesians are known for their beauty and strength. Before the invention of the tractor, they were commonly used for work in the fields.

Rolling is also part of the horses' skin care routine. They usually seek out a dry spot on the ground and, if possible, always return to the same place to roll.

*Friesians are very muscular with a fast trot. In the eighteenth and
nineteenth centuries, they were prized as a fast, fashionable way
to travel. They have boundless energy and strength.*

GLOSSARY

breed — animals having specific traits; to produce offspring.

brow — the forehead.

crossbreeding — mating a male of one breed with a female of another.

croup — the rump of a four-legged animal.

dressage — the art of training a horse to perform certain movements.

foals — newborn male or female horses.

forelock — a lock of hair growing from the front of a horse's head.

gait — a way of walking or running.

gelding — a male horse that has had his reproductive organs removed.

herd — a number of animals of one kind that stay together and travel as a group.

hierarchy — the ranking of individuals within a group from the most to the least powerful.

manes — long hair around the necks of horses.

mares — female horses.

stallions — mature male horses used for breeding.

thoroughbreds — horses and other animals bred from the best blood through a long line.

trot — a four-legged animal's slow running gait.

MORE BOOKS ABOUT HORSES

All About Horses. Marguerite Henry (Random)
Complete Book of Horses and Horsemanship. C. W. Anderson (Macmillan)
The Great Book of Horses. Catherine Dell (R. Rourke)
Guide to the Horses of the World. Caroline Silver (Exeter)
Horse Breeds and Breeding. Jane Kidd (Crescent)
Horse Happy: A Complete Guide to Owning Your Own Horse. Barbara J. Berry (Bobbs-Merrill)
Horses and Riding. George Henschel (Franklin Watts)
Looking At Horses. Jane Behrens (Childrens Press)
The New Complete Book of the Horse. Jane Holderness-Roddam (Smithmark)
The Ultimate Horse Book. Elwyn Hartley Edwards (Dorling Kindersley)
Wild and Wonderful Horses. Cristopher Brown, ed. (Antioch)

VIDEOS

The Art of Riding Series. (Visual Education Productions)
For the Love of Animals: Horse Care and Ownership. (GCG)
Horses! (Encyclopedia Britannica)
The Mare and Foal. (Discovery Trail)
Nature: Wild Horses. (Warner Home Video)

PLACES TO WRITE

Here are some places to write for more information about horses. When you write, include your name and address, and be specific about the information you would like to receive. Don't forget to enclose a stamped, self-addressed envelope for a reply.

National Association for Humane
   and Environmental Education
P.O. Box 362
East Haddam, CT 06423-0362

Horse Council of British Columbia
5746B 176A Street
Cloverdale, British Columbia
V3S 4C7

Pennsylvania Horsebreeder's
   Association
701 East Baltimore Pike, Suite C1
Kennett Square, PA 19348

INDEX